VEILED DREAMS

SHADOWS HAUNTING MY MIND

IANUSI

To my brother, Brihant, for being a constant support and asking me to spare the poor flowers,

Thank you so much for always being there for me.

Contents

Contents

Contents

PREFACE

This book is for all those who think that publishing two books of poetry in a month makes me a certified crackhead.

Wounds

Maana ke hum yaar nahin

Lo tay hai ke pyaar nahin

Phir bhi nazrein na tum milaana

Dil ka aitbaar nahi

I

It feels weird
When the day ends
And you're smiling
Because you're so used to
Crying

II

Today was so...
    Different
    Because I saw a man
    And my first thought wasn't you

III

I think of the last time we met
    There's so much that I should've said
    So much you should've showed
    I was used to being neglected
    So that was never an issue
    It makes me wonder what went away
    But if I had to go back
    And do it all over again
    Perhaps I would steal a kiss first
    And then let fate play its game.

IV

I have filled so many books
    With you
    That perhaps
    When our love changed
    And became hate
    Somewhere it became an obsession

V

Today
    I missed you a little less
    Yet I still try to convince myself
    That if I see you again
    For one last time
    I'll get that closure
    About all that I've left behind
    But even after the 100 imaginary conversations
    I realized
    I still wasn't sure
    That if I were to see you again
    I would hug you
    Or you'd kiss me first

VI

I swear to myself to never fall in love again
   Not after how you screwed me up
   And left,
   But that longing
   And the face that I am looking at
   As I walk down the aisle in my head
   Is always yours
   And I still don't know
   Whether it's something to be scared
   Or to be happy for

VII

I don't know what's more pitiful;
The fact that I am writing poetry again
Or that my muse, even after four books,
It's still you

VIII

I think I imagine you
    Holding the railing of the balcony
    In the middle of the night
    While staring at the only source of light
    Miles away
    Watching me
    And wondering
    About what exactly you did wrong
    I imagine you beating yourself up
    While you see me dance with him
    But instead, there's no him
    And I am watching you
    From miles away
    Carrying her on your back
    Waiting for you to come back
    Wondering where *I* went wrong
    Because I left
    You didn't pursue me
    You replaced me
    In your heart
    And in your home

IX

The forever I could've had with you
I have with your memories
I hallucinate your presence
Or read your old messages
When I feel dead
The ghost of your voice
Is still in my head
Fading fading fading away
But I'm scared
That I'll never hear it again

I am crazy
Because everywhere I go
I see you
I hear your voice
Out loud
And in my head
I fall asleep talking your ghost
But moreover
I smell you wherever I go
And I am crazy
Because I pushed you away
But still need you air.

XI

We always played this game
Where you used to make me guess your smell
Because of how obsessed I was with it
I always thought that I would carry that scent forever
with me
But now I look back
And wish you'd told me
Because day by day
Your memory gets fainter
And I have nothing
But a broken rusty chain
To hold on to

XII

I was so sure that we'd be forever
That I forgot to have a proof
That we existed
I think 60 years later
When I tell my grandkids about you
They'll think that I am crazy
And I think that I am crazy too
Because I took out the shattered pieces of my heart
To fill in the missing spaces of yours
But how will I ever convince them
That even though you loved her
Your heart
Is mine.
Quite literally so.

XIII

I never used to believe
That love and hate could go together
Until I read of Jacks of Hollow
And thought of you
And then read of Ryle
And thought of you again.

XIV

At first, there was only darkness,
Only you, only me
But we ventured out to find
Our stars, our light
And then,
There was only loneliness.

XV

Agony
   Sorrow
   Darkness
   This book you're holding
   Has it all
   Because people are tired
   Of listening me talk about him
   But 4 books later,
   I still am not.

XVI

I think that heartbreak
Is the worst tragedy
Misfortune is up to fate
Death is up to 'God'
But heartbreak
Heartbreak is deliberate
And that is why
It hurts the most

XVII

They force me to believe
   And worship the so called 'God'
   That they fell.
   I ask them, "What God?"
   The one who took it all from me
   Leaving me broken in pieces
   They don't see that I am not
   Just an atheist.
   I am a nihilist
   They took it all from me
   And their God didn't save me

XVIII

No matter how much you tell yourself
   That it is nectar
   If you sip poison
   You will die.

XIX

You ruined me
>For every sunset
>Ever dip
>Every margherita I'll ever sip
>Every movie reminds me
>Of our date
>Every coffee reminds me
>Of our game
>I am utterly, truly ruined
>But just ask
>And I'll still choose you.

XX

I wish I had never met him
    Cause then I would've
    Never moved on from you
    Maybe things would've worked out
    Maybe it would've been the right time
    So screw who says
    Time is always right,
    It's the person who's wrong.
    I don't care if you are right or wrong
    Because you were my person
    And that's all I care for.

XXI

Regrets.
 I never regretted a thing
 Until I met you
 And until I chose you
 Because I know whatever it is
 Ten days or ten months from now
 Whoever I meet or whoever I see
 Will be remind me of you.
 But truth be told,
 You, even you,
 I never regretted you.

XXII

They'll never ever really understand,
    Why I no longer kiss or hold hands
    Why every 'I love you' is responded with
    'As you should'
    And the necklace around my neck
    Is of a rusted hue.
    I tried so hard to fall in love
    To have a muse
    That now,
    I have got you
    In my mind
    In my soul in my body.

I never said 'I love you'
    Until you stopped meaning it
    You never said 'sorry'
    Until I stopped wanting to hear it
    You took me for granted
    Until I actually left.
    I thought you didn't care
    Because you never shared.

XXIV

They say
    You get used to missing someone
    But it had almost been 25 days
    And I miss him more and more
    And the urge to call
    Him gets stronger and stronger
    As I lose myself
    Piece by piece
    Day by day.

XXV

There are so many lonely night
    On which I read our past chats
    I laugh and I cry
    I cry because I miss you
    I miss your voice
    Your stupid smile
    And flirty remarks
    And how much you care.
    And I laugh because just as
    I am about to call you
    I read something so heartbreakingly wrong
    That I remember
    I was as much of your muse as you were mine
    The only difference was that
    You were my poetry
    And I?
    I was your entertainment.

XXVI

There are two kinds of loves in this world
   The ones that last
   And the ones that don't
   You always remained the later
   As much as I begged you to be the former

Scars

Baat chhide jo meri kahin

Tum usko bhool bataa dena

Lekin wo bhool ho aisi

Jis'se bezaar nahin

XXVII

I think one day,
    I'll run out of things to write about you
    One day, I'll open a book
    And the words that I'll pour
    Will be about someone else
    One day,
    I'll think of grief and it won't be cause of you.
    One day,
    I'll have someone else
    To say these words to.

XXVIII

I dread the day I move on from you
But I wonder every day how it will feel
To not have this ache, this longing
These words begging to come out.
How will it feel
To not expect you at the door
Every time a car pulls up.
To not go to the same places
And wonder if what we had was love.

I couldn't fit in a single poem
　　How much you meant to me
　　So I filled five books
　　But you,
　　You could fit in a word how much I meant to you.
　　Sometimes,
　　It was 'everything'
　　And sometimes,
　　It was 'nothing'

XXX

Perhaps, I'll love again
   I am most certain you already have
   But as much as I am scared of being alone
   I am scared of one day waking up
   And not having you in my mind
   Or you not seeing me in every roller coaster ride
   Of me finding a new something old, something blue
   And you finding another set of hands to hold on to.
   Ten years later, would you still think of me at nights?
   Would I still see you in every guy's eyes?

XXXI

Five years later, or perhaps sooner, perhaps later,
    I'll try to convince myself that he's my first love
    I'll erase your existence from my phone
    Perhaps ever my body, my mind, my soul.
    But these books,
    They'll always be the proof of the fact
    That you'll always be the first one.

What do you do
    When your entire personality
    Was determined by one person
    Who you had to leave?
    Who are you then?
    Who am I now,
    When I wake up early
    And do everything that would've made you happy
    Hoping you'd return

XXXIII

It's 2 AM
    And here I am
    Wondering if you're out there
    Trying to forget it all just like I am
    If you agree every time you hear
    You're better off without her
    Or if you say it but don't mean it
    And it that's true, then I don't believe that.
    You stole all my firsts and hung them beside your thirds,
    Like a consolation prize in a hall of honours.
    I made you whole
    Without you, I have no soul.

XXXIV

I moulded myself
To write like you
To speak like you
To act like you
To love what you did
To throw what you didn't
To make sure that every time you looked at me
You saw a home, you say yourself.
Only to find out that you hated yourself.

XXXV

I am scared that one day
You'll wake up and ask,
"She who?"
And as much as I want
My wounds to heal,
I don't want time to do that
Cause if it passes, it will pass for you too.
And honestly,
As much as I want to move on,
I don't want the same for you.
Because I am scared
That the only one who saw me for who I was
Will forget how I looked too.

XXXVI

I force these poems
    To force you out of my body sooner
    To have nothing to write about you any longer
    To not have heartwrenching dreams about you
    And wake up in horror.
    But I know that if I see you tomorrow
    There be force no longer.

XXXVII

I am so glad
    That you hate me as much as I hate you
    Because if I had been the only one
    I don't think I would've been able to stay away.

XXXVIII

"He hates you
    He hates you
    He hates you"
No, you don't hate me
You wish you could hate me
But how can you hate
The only person who wasn't obliged to love you
But still did.

When your life flashes before your eyes
The moment before you die,
I want to be a part of the clip
Even if it is just a glimpse.
I want you to want to live
Just so you could see me again.
I want you to want to live
So we could have the goodbye we never had.
I want you to want to live
For me.

XL

Curse you for having a name
    That is going to haunt me
    For the rest of my life
    I'll hear it in every street I pry.
    Curse you for having a smile
    That I can see on every dace.
    Curse you for having arms
    That I can feel in every embrace.
    Curse you for loving me
    And throwing me away
    Leaving me with wounds
    That I can feel in every place.

XLI

You wanted to make me yours
  And I let you without reading the clause.
  Only later did I realize that out in public I was dirt
  And you were too cool for that, weren't you?
  Then when we were behind locked doors,
  Why did you touch me?
  Why did you cry in my arms and sleep in my lap?
  Why did you make promises that you could've never
kept?

XLII

I told you that I would never leave you
It was a promise.
But when you broke so many of yours,
I realized that promises meant nothing to you.
And I left.

XLIII

You called me cute
    And pulled my cheeks
    Like rubbing the fur
    Of stray cat that you see.
    You never really loved me, no,
    And unlike cats, I didn't boast your serotonin,
    I went for your dopamine.
    And unlike cats, I wasn't your pet,
    I made myself your addiction.

XLIV

Someday, you'll look back
  I am sure of that.
  You'll ask yourself what you did wrong
  And you'll regret.

XLV

You once told me
    That if I were to confess my love for you
    You'd cry
    And not happy tears.
    You'd cry because you would know
    That you would never be able to love me back.

XLVI

I always pretended to forget about your mistakes
  So I could lie to myself
  That you didn't apologize to me
  Because you thought I didn't remember.

XLVII

In another life
    Perhaps we work
    Perhaps we rhyme
    Perhaps we love
    At the same time.
    Perhaps we hope
    Perhaps we pray
    Perhaps we don't
    Set flowers on our own grave.
    Perhaps we match
    The rhymes of our heart
    Perhaps we become more than just art.

XLVIII

True love?
   True love kills
   It hurt
   It stabs you right in the heart
   And it kills
   True love kills

XLIX

I find a muse every time you break my heart
    Only to feel you in every spark
    They might be the blood that runs through my veins
    And blood changes
    But you are my heart
    And the heart is always the same.

# L

You try to replace me over and over again
    But when you learn
    That the soulmate
    Is only one.
    I can scour the earth
    To find peace
    Only to seek it
    Within
    You.

LI

You said you would've never given up
    Unless I asked you
    And I did
    And you did
    Cause we had a happily ever after
    But it was an ending
    An ending of us.

LII

I always wanted them to write a book
   On the broken boy
   And the girl who loved too much
   I always wanted them to make a song
   On the devil
   And the angel who was hurting too much
   I always wanted to see poems
   On the guy who killed
   And the girl who died for love.
   Yet I was in an unmarked grave
   But the dedication to every tragedy ever written.
   They did write a book
   They did made a song
   I did see the poem
   But they failed to be what I was hoping for
   Just like you.

LIII

There's no hole in my heart

But if there were something perhaps it would be a vacuum.

There's no hole in my heart,

For that, my heart would have to exist.

My chest is filled with an organ merely used for oxygenation.

It beats, yes, all alive are not heartless, for then they wouldn't be alive at all.

But if heart were an organ weighing emotions,

A small mythical corner tucked away somewhere at the back of our brain, then no, no, no, I do not been a heart.

I bear a vacuum, sucking in all love given by others, trying to mimic it, trying regenerate it.

But just as a black hole, all I can do is demolish.

LIV

How is it that when I said 'I love you' you couldn't say it back and when you said it, I couldn't mean it?

How is it that we thought that our knives could work as band-aids?

How is it that the ache, and the needed flooded our love until it became a sediment and our longing came out of desperateness?

How is that we took turns loving each other until the masks fell off, leaving us bare to the toxicity?

How is it that our love changed into addiction and slowly killed the two of us?

INTRANSIGENT THOUGHTS

Ianusi

CRIMSON SOLITUDE

Ianusi

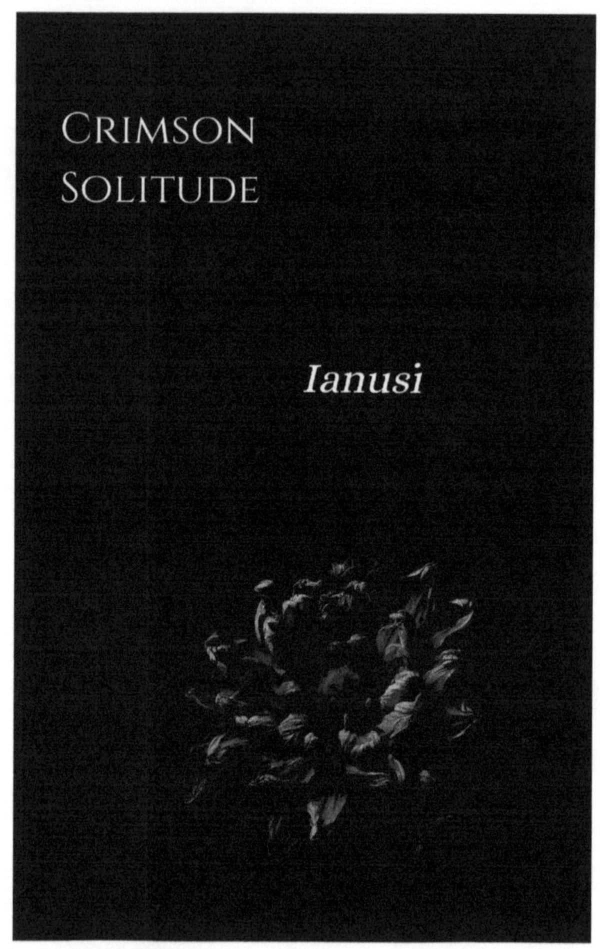

Bleeding Elegies

Ianusi

THE FOURTH BOY

*"My mind succumbs to the urge to
let go"*

IANUSI

Follow me on Instagram @janushi_raichura to get constant updates!